The Best
Enlightenment
Quotes & Passages

To Awaken The Buddha Within

Karin James

ISBN-13: 978-1500309473

ISBN-10: 1500309478

Copyright © 2013 by Karin James

All Rights Reserved. No part of this publication may be reproduced in any form or by any means, including scanning, photocopying, or otherwise without prior written permission of the copyright holder.

First Printing, July 2014
Printed in the United States of America

Contents

Introduction	i
Chapter 1 - Self Inquiry	1
Chapter 2 - Presence	9
Chapter 3 - Thinking	17
Chapter 4 - Silence	24
Chapter 5 - Seeking	29
Chapter 6 - Mystery	37
Chapter 7 - Freedom	44
Chapter 8 - Enlightenment	51
Chapter 9 - Eternal Now	59
Chapter 10 - Non-duality	64
Chapter 11 - Truth	72
Chapter 12 - Illusion	77
Chapter 13 - Fear	83
Chapter 14 - Love	86
Chapter 15 - Suffering	92
Chapter 16 - Death	96
Chapter 17 - Just This	107
Author Index	116

Introduction

Enlightenment is the unshakable knowing that you are the One Reality, as you are, right now and always. It's the unmistakable knowing that there's nothing apart from That, divided from That, separate from That.

It's beyond dogma, belief and faith and can't be approached by these means. It's the non-conceptual recognition that enlightenment is already the case.

There's no becoming in being. It's the complete and utter absence of having anything to do with you or me, because you and me never get enlightened. In fact, an enlightened person never walked this earth. There is no such thing as an enlightened person, so don't expect to become one. It aint' happening.

Enlightenment has nothing to do with the mind and therefore, it has nothing to do with the intellect. So it's best to leave the mind be; this isn't about (or for) the mind. Nonetheless, most will still try to understand the quotes and passages they're about to read.

It's not a state of being, nor is it a state of consciousness. States come and go. Enlightenment does not. It has nothing to do with bliss, but bliss arises in This. It's not an experience among other experiences, but the ever-present substratum that cradles all states and experiences, pleasurable and unpleasurable.

It delights in both, impartially. It doesn't even have a preference. It just welcomes.

There are no steps to enlightenment. Anyone who suggests the notion is simply mistaken. Steps require time and enlightenment is timeless. Besides, steps or a path imply a journey in time becoming something other than what you already are.

Come as you are. Nothing is needed, whatsoever. No journey is necessary, so drop your backpack and kick off your shoes. Sit back and relax, and notice the quiet already present. Go beyond the words to what the words are pointing to. Just don't get stuck on the words.

The finger pointing to the moon isn't the moon, is it? Investigate the notion that you are a separate entity with name and form, here to live for a while only to die. If you give up the need to look for the answers, you may discover that which is beyond answers. You are the silent, aware presence that allows everything to be.

You are the welcoming, space of aware presence that absolutely everything happens in.

Without You, nothing is.

You just forgot.

This is simply You, reminding You, of what You already know.

chapter 1
Self Inquiry

There is no such thing as a person. There are only restrictions and limitations. The sum total of these defines the person. You think you know yourself when you know what you are. But you never know who you are. The person merely appears to be, like the space within the pot appears to have the shape and volume and smell of the pot. Like the space within a pot see that you are not what you believe yourself to be.

Fight with all the strength at your disposal against the idea that you are nameable and describable. You are not. Refuse to think of yourself in terms of this or that. There is no other way out of misery, which you have created for yourself through blind acceptance without investigation. Suffering is a call for enquiry, all pain needs investigation. Don't be too lazy to think.

~ Nisargadatta Maharaj

Enlightenment Quotes & Passages

In recognizing presence awareness, there is no 'thing' to see, just natural, non-conceptual seeing, actually as it is, without subject or object. See this and the realization is immediate that what is labeled as awareness or consciousness or mind can never be formulated as either a subject or an object. Being empty of a subject or object, it is emptiness seeing (cognizing emptiness). Emptiness can never be emptied of emptiness, nor can it be filled by emptiness. With that concept cancelled out, only the wordless, thoughtless indescribable emptiness remains.

Not a vacuum or a void, but a vivid self-shining, self-knowing, self-aware emptiness, like a clear sky full of light. See for yourself. No one or other can do it for you. Immediate simplicity. Continue to see that the seeing is continuous. Any doubt, question, or argument, and the conceptual seeker has appeared again. See that and non-conceptual emptiness remains undisturbed.

~ Sailor Bob Adamson

If you cannot find truth where you are, where do you expect to find it?

~ Dogen

I 'exist' is the only permanent self-evident experience of everyone. Nothing else is so self-evident as 'I am'. What people call self-evident, that is, the experience they get through the senses, is far from self-evident. The Self alone is that. So to do self-enquiry and be that 'I am' is the only thing to do. 'I am' is reality. I am this or that is unreal. 'I am' is truth, another name for Self.

~ Ramana Maharshi

In oneself lies the whole world and if you know how to look and learn, the door is there and the key is in your hand. Nobody on earth can give you either the key or the door to open, except yourself.

~ Jiddu Krishnamurti

Just realize you are dreaming a dream you call the world and stop looking for ways out. The dream is not your problem. Your problem is that you like one part of your dream and not another. Love all or none of it, and stop complaining.

Enlightenment Quotes & Passages

When you have seen the dream as a dream, you have done all that needs to be done.

~ Nisargadatta Maharaj

Has it ever occurred to you that you are seeking God with His eyes?

~ Adyashanti

What I have to offer is very simple. It has nothing to do with acquiring any special powers or any state of mind. It is about recognizing what is already permanently here, in every moment, every situation, and every state of mind, and yet is ungraspable by the mind.

~ Gangaji

The root of all desires is the one desire: to come home, to be at peace. There may be a moment in life when our compensatory activities, the accumulation of money, learning and objects, leave us feeling deeply apathetic. This can motivate us towards the search for our real nature beyond appearances. We may find ourselves asking, 'Why am I here? What is life? Who am I?' Sooner or later any intelligent person asks these questions.

~ Jean Klein

The most intimate question we can ask, and the one that has the most spiritual power, is this: What or who am I?

~ Adyashanti

The mind will merge only by Self-enquiry 'Who am I?' The thought 'Who am I?' will destroy all other thoughts and finally kill itself also. If other thoughts arise, without trying to complete them, one must enquire to whom did this thought arise. What does it matter how many thoughts arise?

As each thought arises one must be watchful and ask to whom is this thought occurring. The answer will be 'to me'. If you enquire 'Who am I?' the mind will return to its source (or where it issued from). The thought which arose will also submerge. As you practice like this more and more, the power of the mind to remain as its source is increased.

~ Ramana Maharshi

Enlightenment Quotes & Passages

Look within, there is no difference between yourself, Self and Guru.

You are always Free.

There is no teacher, there is no student, there is no teaching.

~Papaji

You know, if we understand one question rightly, all questions are answered. But we don't know how to ask the right question. To ask the right question demands a great deal of intelligence and sensitivity. Here is a question, a fundamental question: is life a torture?

It is, as it is; and man has lived in this torture centuries upon centuries, from ancient history to the present day, in agony, in despair, in sorrow; and he doesn't find a way out of it. Therefore he invents gods, churches, all the rituals, and all that nonsense, or he escapes in different ways. What we are trying to do, during all these discussions and talks here, is to see if we cannot radically bring about a transformation of the mind, not accept things as they are, nor revolt against them.

Revolt doesn't answer a thing. You must understand it, go into it, examine it, give your heart and your mind, with everything that you have, to find out a way of living differently. That depends on you, and not on someone else, because in this there is no teacher, no pupil; there is no leader; there is no guru; there is no Master, no Savior. You yourself are the teacher and the pupil; you are the Master; you are the guru; you are the leader; you are everything. And to understand is to transform what is.

~ Jiddu Krishnamurti

The Self always is. There is no knowing it. It is not some new knowledge to be acquired. What is new and not here and now cannot be permanent. The Self always is, but knowledge of it is obstructed and the obstruction is called ignorance. Remove the ignorance and knowledge shines forth. In fact, it is not the Self that has this ignorance or even knowledge. These are only accretions to be cleared away That is why the Self is said to be beyond knowledge and ignorance.

All doubts will cease only when the doubter and his source have been found. It is no use endlessly removing doubts. If we clear up one another will arise and there will be no end to them. But if the doubter himself is found to be really nonexistent by seeking his source, then all doubts will cease. It remains as it naturally is--that is all.

~ Ramana Maharshi

chapter 2
Presence

You might be looking at a mountain, and you have relaxed into the effortlessness of your present awareness, and then suddenly the mountain is all, you are nothing. Your separate-self sense is suddenly and totally gone, and there is simply everything that is arising moment to moment. You are perfectly aware, perfectly conscious, everything seems completely normal, except you are nowhere to be found. You are not on this side of your face looking at the mountain out there; you simply are the mountain, you are the sky, you are the clouds, you are everything that is arising moment to moment, very simply, very clearly, just so.

~ Ken Wilber

Enlightenment Quotes & Passages

Basically, there is nothing apart from the presence-awareness that you are right now. All seeking and understanding comes back to the seeing of this. Approaching this involves no time, path or practice. And, contrary to popular belief, there is no deepening or improving. Nor is there any need for awakening for embodying. What you are is fully awake and present now. Since there is no individual, as such, there is no one who needs to embody anything or bring the understanding into life. There is nothing to surrender or let go of because there is really no one or nothing present that can do any such thing. It is just a simple recognition of the obvious that was over looked. This is about it in a nutshell.

~ John Wheeler

In truth, there is no Seer or Witness; there is simply Seeing, Witnessing--and You Are That. There is something that notices the silent seer or witness. Like light, it cannot itself be seen, and yet it illuminates all that is seen. We can't say it is absent, but it can never be found. This is the mystery of being conscious.

~ David A. Bhodan

Self is what you are. You are That Fathomlessness in which experience and concepts appear.

Self is the Moment that has no coming or going. It is the Heart, Atman, Emptiness. It shines to Itself, by Itself, in Itself.

Self is what gives breath to Life. You need not search for It, It is Here. You are That through which you would search.

You *are* what you are looking for! And That is All it is. Only Self is.

~ Papaji

Our minds turn awakening into a task. We feel it is something that we have to do, which is true up to a point, but we shouldn't intimidate ourselves with that. Actually, realizing the Truth becomes a kind of joy and effortlessness, and gradually we find it is just confirming itself by itself.

Already it has presented itself in some subtle way within you. You cannot be bored with it, if it is truly alive. Instead of pushing, just be more quiet and let it continue to show itself. Let it find its natural way to reveal itself. Just let it come.

Enlightenment Quotes & Passages

Your place is to stay inside the heart: Yes, absorb me! There is tremendous power in this, when genuinely expressed.

~ Mooji

Our true nature is that simple and undeniable presence of awareness that illumines all thinking feeling and perceiving. Always present and radiantly clear, it is never obscured by time, circumstances or thoughts.

The body, mind and world rise and set in awareness and have no independent existence apart from awareness. Awareness, your real being, is all there is. You are not the limited person you have taken yourself to be. Look for the separate self and you find it entirely absent. Seeing this, suffering, doubt and confusion effortlessly drop away, revealing your nature of innate happiness and freedom. Understanding who you are is immediate and always available-- here and now!

~ John Wheeler

Sit, then, as if you were a mountain, with all the unshakeable, steadfast majesty of a mountain.

A mountain is completely natural and at ease with itself, however strong the winds that try to bother it, however thick the dark clouds that swirl around its peak. Sitting like a mountain, let your mind rise and fly and soar.

~ Sogyal Rinpoche

Presence, being, awareness, your true nature and so on, all refer to the same thing, which is no thing. Seeing, hearing, thinking, feeling and all else arise within or appear on this cognizing emptiness that you are. Under no circumstance can you doubt your own being. The mind cannot understand this, know this or sense this in any way, because the mind appears in this. Yet, it is intimately and clearly known at all times. It is going on all the time, but we miss it or overlook it because it is so clear and obvious.

There has never been any ego or person or separate entity. If you think there is, then look for it and try to find it. Other than passing thoughts, feelings and sensations, is there any substantial entity that you can call yourself? See this and your seeking is done.

Everything arises and appears within this presence that is your true being. As such, it is all made of the same substance, your true nature. It is all that, and you are that. So what do you need to attain or understand? Once this is pointed out, it simply sinks in and resonates. The result is that all questions, doubts and suffering are gone for good.

~ John Wheeler

The Reality is not the pain. The body is in pain, but you are not the body. So if you stick to your true self, you will hardly feel the pain. Let the body take care of itself. Do not concern yourself with the body. The body will still eat, it will still go to the bathroom, it will still take a shower, it will still take care of itself, but you have absolutely nothing to do with it. You are not the body, so why identify with the pain. Identify with consciousness, with the self, and then see what happens.

~ Robert Adams

Rather than going after these walls and barriers with a sledgehammer, we pay attention to them. With gentleness and honesty, we move closer to those walls. We touch them, and smell them and get to know them well.

We become familiar with the strategies and beliefs we use to build these walls: what are the stories

To Awaken The Buddha Within

we tell ourselves? What repels me and what attracts me? Without calling what we see right or wrong, we simply look as objectively as we can.

We can observe ourselves with humor, not getting overly serious, moralistic or uptight about the investigation. Year after year, we train in remaining open and receptive to whatever arises. Slowly, very slowly, the cracks in the walls seem to widen and, as if by magic, Bodhichitta is able to flow freely.

~ Pema Chodron

When you relate to thoughts obsessively, you are actually feeding them because thoughts need your attention to survive. Once you begin to pay attention to them and categorize them, then they become very powerful. You are feeding them energy because you are not seeing them as simple phenomena. If one tries to quiet them down, that is another way of feeding them.

~ Chogyam Trungpa

We feel we sometimes lose or leave this. But this 'I who leaves' is the mind only--a thought. How can we Leave our Self? Can the wave (the mind) exist apart from the ocean (the

Enlightenment Quotes & Passages

Self)? 'Losing and gaining' are simply notions arising in the Unchanging presence we already are.

~ Mooji

When you meditate, do not try to have good thoughts, do not try to keep away bad thoughts, do not try to stop thoughts, and do not try to go after them. Rather, rest in a state of being aware of the thoughts as they arise.

~ Kalu Rinpoche

chapter 3
Thinking

In the sky, there is no distinction of east and west; people create distinctions out of their own minds and then believe them to be true.

~ Buddha

All the world's a stage, and all the men and women merely players. There is nothing either good or bad but thinking makes it so. Life is a tale told by an idiot, full of sound and fury, signifying nothing. I say there is no darkness but ignorance. To thine own Self be true and it must follow as the night the day, thou canst not then be false to any man. There are more things in heaven and earth than are dreamt of in your philosophy.

Enlightenment Quotes & Passages

Life's but a walking shadow, a poor player that struts and frets his hour upon a stage.

~ Shakespeare

Not knowing our true nature, which is peace itself, we have turned to the mind for answers. The mind has provided all kinds of ideas and concepts about who we are and what is the way to peace. It is through ignorance that the innate desire for happiness keeps us focused on thoughts.

In discovering our true nature, there is a profound shift of experience because we tap directly into the source of peace, clarity and certitude. Then the focus on the mind naturally falls off because we see that it is not delivering the freedom, which is now our direct experience. Without this understanding, trying to get free of the mind is pretty much an exercise of futility.

~ John Wheeler

Even if you have not awakened, if you realize that your perceptions and activities are all like dreams and you view them with detachment, not giving rise to grasping and rejecting discrimination, then this is virtually tantamount to awakening from the dream.

~ Muso Kokushi

Really, what we are has nothing to do with still minds, death of egos, purification or any of the ideas we have been taught about states we should be in. This kind of teaching has to do with personal predispositions. It's always attractive to the mind when it is offered a method or a technique like stilling the mind or killing the ego.

There is no possibility for the mind to still the mind, and once it is recognized that what you are is the still, silent awareness that sees the mind and its activities going on, then it is also recognized that there is no need to still the mind. It's all very simple, really--what we are is just the background, just sitting there waiting for us to stop somewhere and see the busyness. Once this happens, then we begin to have a different taste about what we are.

~ Tony Parsons

There is one mind common to all individual men. Every man is an inlet to the same and to all of the same. He that is once admitted to the right of reason is made a freeman of the whole estate. What Plato has thought, he may think; what a saint has felt, he may feel; what at any time has be-fallen any man, he can understand. Who hath access to this universal mind is a party to all that is or can be done, for this is the only and sovereign agent.

~ Ralph Waldo Emerson

The realm of consciousness is much vaster than thought can grasp. When you no longer believe everything you think, you step out of thought and see clearly that the thinker is not who you are.

~ Eckhart Tolle

Put your awareness to work, not your mind. The mind is not the right instrument for this task. The timeless can be reached only by the timeless. Your body and your mind are born subject to time; only awareness is timeless, even in the now. You may die a hundred deaths without a break in the mental turmoil. Or, you may keep your body and die only in the mind. The death of the mind is the birth of wisdom.

~ Nisargadatta Maharaj

Recognize the power of mind, respect the power of mind. And also recognize the power behind the power, the ocean holding the wave Recognize yourself as the ocean, with your stories, your feelings, as waves. Waves can be beautiful or terrifying, but always they return to the ocean. Every wave always is made up of the ocean. No wave can ever be separate from the ocean. Waves of thoughts, waves of emotions, waves of sensations, waves of events, are all made up of consciousness. And all return to consciousness, while never being separate from consciousness. And if this becomes another story, let this go, and see what is true.

~ Gangaji

Be the witness of your thoughts. You are what observes, not what you observe.

~ Buddha

You were here before you were born, and you will be here after you are dead. The mind has a very limited existence, very momentary--one day it comes, another day it is gone. You are forever. Have some experience of your foreverness. But that is possible only through no-mind. No-mind is another name for meditation.

~Osho

The mind may accept or deny that you are awareness, but either way it can't really understand. It cannot comprehend. Thought cannot comprehend what is beyond thought.

~ Adyashanti

If there were nothing but thought in you, you wouldn't even know you are thinking. You would be like a dreamer who doesn't know he is dreaming. When you know you are dreaming, you are awake within the dream.

~ Eckhart Tolle

Subject-object thinking seems to cover the natural state (awareness). But without awareness, thinking could not take place. Because thinking appears in awareness (like a cloud appears in the sky), realize that thinking in essence is awareness. Understanding this, thinking cannot obscure awareness.

To Awaken The Buddha Within

~ Sailor Bob Adamson

The mind is restless with the urge to accomplish or become. You cannot reach or become Beingness, for Beingness is already what you are. Rest in that as that. Enjoy and be fulfilled in this knowing. This is real knowledge, satisfaction and contentment.

~ Mooji

As soon as you see something, you already start to intellectualize it. As soon as you intellectualize something, it is no longer what you saw.

~ Shunryu Suzuki

chapter 4
Silence

It is only through silent awareness that our physical and mental nature can change. This change is completely spontaneous. If we make an effort to change we do no more than shift our attention from one level, from one thing, to another. We remain in a vicious circle. This only transfers energy from one point to another. It still leaves us oscillating between suffering and pleasure, each leading inevitably back to the other. Only living stillness, stillness without someone trying to be still, is capable of undoing the conditioning our biological, emotional and psychological nature has undergone.

There is no controller, no selector, no personality making choices. In choice-less living the situation is given the freedom to unfold. You do not grasp one aspect over another for there is nobody to grasp. When you understand something and live it without being stuck to the formulation, what you have understood dissolves in your openness. In this silence change takes place of its own accord, the problem is resolved and duality ends. You are left in your glory where no one has understood and nothing has been understood.

~ Jean Klein

Be still and know yourself as the Truth you have been searching for. Be still and let the inherent joy of that Truth capture your drama and destroy it in the bliss of consummation. Be still and let your life be lived by the purpose you were made for. Be still and receive the inherent truth of your heart.

~ Gangaji

To the mind that is still, the whole universe surrenders.

~ Lao Tzu

Enlightenment Quotes & Passages

Bibles may convey and priests expound, but it is exclusively for the noiseless operation of one's own Self, to enter the pure ether of veneration, reach the divine levels and commune with the unutterable.

~ Walt Whitman

Something is bound. And then there is something that is already free. You must differentiate which one you are. Shed this tight costume of personality and slip into your timeless Being. Just feel that 'stuff', allow it to be expressed, it flows within the human expression of consciousness, let it be.

Because when it has been given the room to express itself, then the space behind, which is joyful, steady and tranquil will come to the front, only don't name this enlightenment and then feel that you've gained something; instead recognize and pay full attention to the unchanging silence which is the substratum of all that is appearing in the mind.

~ Mooji

To Awaken The Buddha Within

There is only timeless Being, the inexplicable mystery of what you are.

You are both the Source and Essence of all, always, already, without any condition.

Resting as unchanging awareness, peace and joy, You manifest as all changing worlds and beings.

There is no requirement to be what you are. Instead, simply be what you are.

There is no effort needed to see what is actually here. What effort is needed to arrive at the effortless?

Let go of the assumption you are a limited body/mind possessed with a particular lifespan.

In the silence of awareness that you are, turn 180-degrees around and face your Self, surrender the 'I' thought and see you've always been free.

Recognize it's all been a dream that happened to no one.

I am the silence in the song and the song in the silence. And it sings so beautifully.

~ David A. Bhodan

Enlightenment Quotes & Passages

In a mind clear as still water, even the waves, breaking, are reflecting its light.

~ Dogen

A quiet mind is all you need. All else will happen rightly, once your mind is quiet. As the sun on rising makes the world active, so does self-awareness affect changes in the mind. In the light of calm and steady self-awareness inner energies wake up and work miracles without effort on your part.

~ Nisargadatta Maharaj

All is perfection only. Perfection is everywhere to behold; But first you must have the eyes to see it. Only the one with perfect eyes can see Perfection. Think of yourself, and a subtle image is formed inside the mind. You are not this nor any image or thought.

You are the Silent and formless Awareness within which innumerable impressions appear and disappear without trace.

~ Mooji

chapter 5
Seeking

There seem to be two kinds of searchers: those who seek to make their ego something other than it is, i.e. holy, happy, unselfish (as though you could make a fish unfish), and those who understand that all such attempts are just gesticulation and play-acting, that there is only one thing that can be done, which is to disidentify themselves with the ego, by realizing its unreality, and by becoming aware of their eternal identity with pure being.

~ Wei Wu Wei

The Master made it his task to destroy systematically every doctrine, every belief, every concept of the divine, for these things, which were originally intended as pointers, were now being taken as descriptions. He loved to quote the Eastern saying 'When the sage points to the moon, all that the idiot sees is the finger'.

~ Anthony de Mello

Now don't think that awakening is the end. Awakening is the end of seeking, the end of the seeker, but it is the beginning of a life lived from your true nature.

~ Adyashanti

The very desire to seek spiritual enlightenment is in fact nothing but the grasping tendency of the ego itself, and thus the very search for enlightenment prevents it. The 'perfect practice' is therefore not to search for enlightenment, but to inquire into the motive for seeking itself.

You obviously seek in order to avoid the present, and yet the present alone holds the answer: to seek forever is to miss the point forever. You always already are enlightened Spirit, and therefore to seek Spirit is simply to deny Spirit.

To Awaken The Buddha Within

You can no more attain Spirit than you can attain your feet or acquire your lungs.

~ Ken Wilber

Seekers continue to practice all kinds of self-torture without realizing that such 'spiritual practice' is a reinforcement of the very ego that prevents them from their natural, free state.

~ Ramesh Balsekar

Trying to find a Buddha or enlightenment is like trying to grab space.

~ Bodhidharma

Many spiritual seekers get 'stuck' in emptiness, in the absolute, in transcendence. They cling to bliss, or peace, or indifference. When the self-centered motivation for living disappears, many seekers become indifferent. They see the perfection of all existence and find no reason for doing anything, including caring for themselves or others. I call this 'taking a false refuge.' It is a very subtle egoic trap; it's a fixation in the absolute and all unconscious form of attachment that masquerades as liberation. It can be very difficult to wake someone up from this deceptive fixation because they literally have no motivation to let go of it. Stuck in a form of divine indifference, such people believe they have reached the top of the mountain when actually they are hiding out halfway up its slope.

Enlightenment does not mean one should disappear into the realm of transcendence. To be fixated in the absolute is simply the polar opposite of being fixated in the relative. With the dawning of true enlightenment, there is a tremendous birthing of impersonal Love and wisdom that never fixates in any realm of experience. To awaken to the absolute view is profound and transformative, but to awaken from all fixed points of view is the birth of true non-duality. If emptiness cannot dance, it is not true Emptiness. If moonlight does not flood the empty night sky and reflect in every drop of water, on every blade of grass, then you are only looking at your own empty dream.

I say, Wake up! Then, your heart will be flooded with a Love that you cannot contain.

~ Adyashanti

There is no greater mystery than this, that we keep seeking reality though in fact we are reality. 'We' think that there is something hiding reality and that this must be destroyed before reality is gained. How ridiculous! A day will dawn when you will laugh at all your past efforts. That which will be the day you laugh is also here and now.

~ Ramana Maharshi

Why should I seek? I am the same as he. His essence speaks through me. I have been looking for myself.

~ Rumi

If you are seeking do you even really know what it is that you seek? Is it truth, or is it just wanting to feel good? Most people run a mile when they actually hear the Truth because it undermines the very ground that you think you are standing on.

~ Unmani

Enlightenment Quotes & Passages

What is sought remains hidden from the seeker by already being everything. It is so obvious and simple that the grasping of it obscures it. Never found, never knowable, being is the consummate absence that is beyond measure.

Looking for being is believing it is lost. Has anything been lost, or is it simply that the looking keeps it away? Does the beloved always dance constantly just beyond our serious focus?

The very intention to seek for a mythical treasure within life inevitably obscures the reality that life is already the treasure.

~ Tony Parsons

In truth, everything and everyone is a shadow of the Beloved and our seeking is His seeking. And our words are His words.

We search for Him here and there while looking right at Him.

Sitting by His side, we ask: 'O Beloved, where is the Beloved'?

~ Rumi

In short, the imaginary separate self is always seeking peace, happiness and love in an outside object, other or world. However, the separate self cannot find peace, happiness and love because its apparent existence is the veiling of it. At the same time peace, happiness and love is all the separate self seeks.

All separate selves seek only the end of seeking; all separate selves long only for the end of longing; all separate selves desire only to dissolve or die. That death--the death of the separate self--'is' the experience of peace, happiness and love, the unveiling of our essential nature, its 'remembering' of itself.

However, as we have seen, the separate self is only a real self from its own illusory point of view. How can an illusion die if it is not real to begin with? It cannot! It can only be seen to be utterly non-existent.

If the separate self were real it would be impossible to get rid of it because that which is real cannot disappear. And fortunately, that which is unreal, such as a separate self, object, other or world, never truly comes into existence.

Enlightenment Quotes & Passages

Therefore, no activity or cessation of the mind's activity can bring about this understanding. All that is required is to have the courage, honesty and love to look, to see clearly, and to live the implications of what we discover.

~ Rupert Spira

chapter 6
Mystery

The genius of a composer is found in the notes of his music; but analyzing the notes will not reveal his genius.

The poet's greatness is contained in his words; yet the study of his words will not disclose his inspiration.

God reveals himself in creation; but scrutinize creation as minutely as you wish, you will not find God, any more than you will find the soul through careful examination of your body.

~ Anthony de Mello

Water has no shape; its nature is to flow. If you put it into a vase it will take the shape of the vase. In this cup, it has assumed the shape of the cup. If poured it into my cupped hands it will take the shape of the hands.

But water has no shape. It is the same with the consciousness, which is subtler than water. It similarly has no form, but it assumes the form of whatever concept it is poured into or identifies with, but it will never be the form. It remains ever its formless nature.

~ Mooji

If you begin to understand what you are without trying to change it, then what you are undergoes a transformation.

~ Jiddu Krishnamurti

A living body is not a fixed thing but a flowing event, like a flame or a whirlpool: the shape alone is stable, for the substance is a stream of energy going in at one end and out at the other. We are particularly and temporarily identifiable wiggles in a stream that enters us in the form of light, heat, air, water, milk, bread, fruit, beer, beef stroganoff, caviar, and pate de foie gras. It goes out as gas and excrement--and also as semen, babies, talk, politics, commerce, war, poetry, music and philosophy.

~ Alan Watts

He who experiences the unity of life sees his own Self in all beings, and all beings in his own Self, and looks on everything with an impartial eye.

~ Buddha

You are divine at centre, human in appearance at a certain range. Seeing who you really are doesn't mean you are no longer aware of your appearance, no longer self-conscious--that's impossible as well as undesirable.

So you still respond to your name, still recognize yourself in the mirror, still take responsibility for your actions. Of course. But you are now aware that your humanity is like a disguise, an incarnation you have taken on to be here in this world. Inwardly you are God, outwardly you are a person--a unique person with a special contribution to make.

Instead of thinking you are just that person, that appearance, you are awake to the Power behind you, the Safety within you, the Source of inspiration and guidance at the heart of your human life. This enables you to be yourself even more so.

~ Douglas Harding

I cannot be awake for nothing looks to me as it did before, or else I am awake for the first time, and all before has been a mean sleep.

~ Walt Whitman

Not Christian or Jew or Muslim, not Hindu, Buddhist, Sufi, or Zen. Not any religion or cultural system.

I am not from the East or the West, not out of the ocean or up from the ground, not natural or ethereal, not composed of elements at all.

I do not exist, am not an entity in this world or in the next did not descend from Adam and Eve or any origin story. My place is placeless, a trace of the traceless. Neither body or soul.

To Awaken The Buddha Within

I belong to the beloved, have seen the two worlds as one and that one call to and know, first, last, outer, inner, only that breath breathing human being.

~ Rumi

You are the sky. Everything else--it's just the weather.

~ Pema Chodron

Life will give you whatever experience is most helpful for the evolution of your consciousness. How do you know this is the experience you need? Because this is the experience you are having at the moment.

~ Eckhart Tolle

At the center of your being you have the answer; you know who you are and you know what you want.

~ Lao Tzu

Enlightenment Quotes & Passages

As you make more and more powerful microscopic instruments, the universe has to get smaller and smaller in order to escape the investigation. Just as when the telescopes become more and more powerful, the galaxies have to recede in order to get away from the telescopes. Because what is happening in all these investigations is this: Through us and through our eyes and senses, the universe is looking at itself. And when you try to turn around to see your own head, what happens? It runs away. You can't get at it. This is the principle. Shankara explains it beautifully in his commentary on the Kenopanishad where he says 'That which is the Knower, the ground of all knowledge, is never itself an object of knowledge.

~ Alan Watts

To locate a thing you need space, to place an event you need time; but the timeless and space-less defies handling.

It makes everything perceivable, yet itself is beyond perception. The mind cannot know what is beyond the mind, but the mind is known by what is beyond it.

~ Nisargadatta Maharaj

To Awaken The Buddha Within

As long as there is a 'you' doing or not doing, thinking or not-thinking, meditating or not-meditating, you are no closer to home than the day you were born.

~ Wei Wu Wei

Events happen, deeds are done, but there is no doer thereof.

~ Buddha

Through our eyes, the universe is perceiving itself. Through our ears, the universe is listening to its harmonies. We are the witnesses through which the universe becomes conscious of its glory, of its magnificence.

~ Alan Watts

chapter 7
Freedom

Leave everything outside and come in. Everything you see, you must leave. Don't want anything, not even enlightenment. Everyone can do this. Come right into that place before all these things were formed. Allow yourself to be undone of all falsehood. Then you will discover for yourself that emptiness that has never moved: Everything else has moved. This is your ground. The ground of Being; your very Self is That.

~ Mooji

I start out on this road, call it Love or Emptiness. I only know what's not here.

Resentment seeds, back scratching greed, worrying about outcome, fear of people.

To Awaken The Buddha Within

When a bird gets free, it does not go back for remnants left on the bottom of the cage.

Close by, I'm rain. Far off, a cloud of fire. I seem restless, but I am deeply at ease.

Branches tremble. The roots are still. I am a universe in a handful of dirt, whole when totally demolished.

Talk about choices does not apply to me. While intelligence considers options, I Am Somewhere Lost In The Wind.

~ Rumi

To know the self as the only reality and all else as temporal and transient is freedom, peace and joy. It is all very simple. Instead of seeing things as imagined, learn to see them as they are.

When you can see everything as it is, you will also see yourself as you are. It is like cleansing a mirror. The same mirror that shows you the world as it is will also show you your own face.

The thought 'I am' is the polishing cloth. Use it.

~ Nisargadatta Maharaj

Enlightenment Quotes & Passages

When you shift your identity from your self-image to your true Self, you will find happiness that no one can take away from you.

~ Deepak Chopra

Remember, freedom is not attained, especially by some imagined 'I' trying to get it. It is the recognition that what you are (as the undeniable sense of presence) has never been bound. Stick with the basics. Awareness is naturally detached because it is the unchanging background of all appearances. Yet it is certainly not aloof. It is the source and substance of everyone and everything in the manifestation.

~ John Wheeler

In Freedom there is no right and wrong. In Freedom there is freedom from right and wrong.

In Freedom there is no process or way, no here, no there, no this, no that, no in, no out, no wall, no depth, no understanding.

Nothing has happened, nothing is happening, nothing ever will happen. No mind, no bondage, no freedom.

In Wisdom there is no phenomena, there is no giver and no receiver and so life is very beautiful, the world is very beautiful, and relationships are very beautiful because they are all with your Self. The Supreme is concealed by name and form but when the Truth is known, It will conceal name and form.

~ Papaji

What a liberation to realize that the 'voice in my head' is not who I am. Who am I then? The one who sees that.

~ Eckhart Tolle

This being human is a guest house. Every morning a new arrival. A joy, a depression, a meanness, some momentary awareness comes as an unexpected visitor.

Welcome and entertain all! Even if they're a crowd of sorrows, who violently sweep your house empty of its furniture, still, treat each guest honorably. He may be clearing you out for some new delight.

The dark thought, the shame, the malice, meet them at the door laughing, and invite them in. Be

Enlightenment Quotes & Passages

grateful for whomever comes, because each has been sent as a guide from beyond.

~ Rumi

I am...the divine expression exactly as I am, right here, right now. You are the divine expression exactly as you are, right here, right now. Nothing, absolutely nothing, needs to be added or taken away. Nothing is more valid or sacred than anything else. No conditions need to be filled. The infinite is not somewhere else waiting for us to become worthy.

The life story that has apparently happened is uniquely and exactly appropriate for each awakening. All is just as it should be, right now. Not because it is a potential for something better, but simply because all that is, is divine expression.

~ Tony Parsons

What is liberation? It is to be free of personal identity. It is to be free from the hypnosis of conditioning; to be free from the magnetic influence and compulsiveness of the psychological mind.

It is to recognize that you are not an object, that this body is an inadequate representation of being, and is only a vessel through which consciousness and the vital force act in their portrayal called 'life'.

~ Mooji

Recognize the naturalness that you are--pure, all pervasive, space like, ever expressing, spontaneous presence awareness, with no reference point (self nature) having any substance or independent existence.

Failing to recognize naturalness (the unity of appearance and emptiness, space and its content), delusion happens and there is a grasping of or fixation on appearance--me and the other--a seeming duality.

Without that fixation there is freedom as naturalness, delusion dissolves and evenness (non-duality) remains--the natural state--simply this, nothing else.

Naturally remaining as naturalness (equanimity) is the natural (effortless) meditation of no one to meditate and nothing to meditate on--no trying to get or trying to avoid, just effortless being which is

Enlightenment Quotes & Passages

always already so.

Recognize this again and again.

~ Sailor Bob Adamson

Try to remember the main points: Birth and death are like going to sleep at night and waking up in the morning. When you go to sleep at night, you die, when you dream it's like being on an astral plane, and when you wake up in the morning, it's like being born. Through those states of consciousness somebody exists, and that somebody is none other than you.

In other words you are aware of dreaming. You are aware of sleeping. You are aware of waking up. You are aware of dying, and you are aware of being reborn. Somebody is watching all this, that's you. You exist through all those states. Abide in your existence, not in the states. Ignore the fake consciousness. Abide in the reality, which is called absolute awareness, consciousness. Abide in that and be free.

~ Robert Adams

chapter 8
Enlightenment

Enlightenment is the sudden realization that non-duality, not duality, is the reality of our experience. Consciousness is not private and personal, but universal and impersonal, eternally.

~ David A. Bhodan

Enlightenment is like the moon reflected on the water. The moon does not get wet, nor is the water broken. Although its light is wide and great, the moon is reflected even in a puddle an inch wide. The whole moon and the entire sky are reflected in dewdrops on the grass, or even in one drop of water.

Enlightenment does not divide you, just as the moon does not break the water. You cannot hinder enlightenment, just as a drop of water does not hinder the moon in the sky. The depth of the drop is the height of the moon. Each reflection, however long or short its duration, manifests the vastness of the dewdrop, and realizes the limitlessness of the moonlight in the sky.

~ Dogen

We assume we will awaken to something else, something bigger and more grand. But really it is awakening to yourself, to what is here, has always been here. That is the startling, refreshing, wonderful, good news.

~ Gangaji

Do not think that enlightenment is going to make you special, it's not. If you feel special in any way, then enlightenment has not occurred. I meet a lot of people who think they are enlightened and awake simply because they have had a very moving spiritual experience. They wear their enlightenment on their sleeve like a badge of honor. They sit among friends and talk about how awake they are while sipping coffee at a cafe. The funny thing about enlightenment is that when it is authentic, there is no one to claim it. Enlightenment is very ordinary; it is nothing special. Rather than making you more special, it is going to make you less special. It plants you right in the center of a wonderful humility and innocence. Everyone else may or may not call you enlightened, but when you are enlightened the whole notion of enlightenment and someone who is enlightened is a big joke.

I use the word enlightenment all the time; not to point you toward it but to point you beyond it. Do not get stuck in enlightenment.

~ Adyashanti

Enlightenment is finding that there is nothing to find. Enlightenment is to come to know that there is nowhere to go. Enlightenment is the understanding that this is all, that this is perfect, that this is it. Enlightenment is not an achievement, it is an understanding that there is nothing to achieve, nowhere to go. You are already there-- you have never been away. You cannot be away from there. God has never been missed.

Maybe you have forgotten, that's all. Maybe you have fallen asleep, that's all.

~ Osho

Enlightenment Quotes & Passages

In the process of burning out these confusions, we discover enlightenment. If the process were otherwise, the awakened state of mind would be a product dependent upon cause and effect and therefore liable to dissolution. Anything which is created must, sooner or later, die. If enlightenment were created in such a way, there would always be a possibility of ego reasserting itself, causing a return to the confused state. Enlightenment is permanent because we have not produced it; we have merely discovered it.

~ Chogyam Trungpa

All the Buddha's of all the ages have been telling you a very simple fact: Be--don't try to become. Within these two words, be and becoming, your whole life is contained. Being is enlightenment, becoming is ignorance.

~ Osho

Enlightenment appears to come in stages, but in Truth, it happens all at once when it happens. Awakening happens suddenly, like when you turn on a light bulb in the darkness. The darkness immediately disappears. When you turn on your own light, maya, ignorance, disappears. You are home. It happens when you don't want it to happen. As long as you want it to happen there is somebody who wants it to happen. That somebody has to disappear. The person that wants it to happen is keeping you back. That is the personal I. Silence is the best way to wake up.

~ Robert Adams

Enlightenment is not something you achieve. It is the absence of something. All your life you have been going forward after something, pursuing some goal. Enlightenment is dropping all that.

~ Charlotte J. Beck

Awareness is all there is. You are Awareness Itself, not somebody who is aware. Enlightenment is rather simple. It's really nothing more than remembering something forgotten. It is nothing more, or other than, the realization of the true nature of Reality.

Liberation is the spontaneous cognition and remembrance that separation and individuality are both illusory. Enlightenment knows the mind is an object in awareness, an appearance on the screen of the Changeless Reality you are.

Enlightenment Quotes & Passages

Enlightenment is the absence of any separate individual entity we call a person. Therefore, no one becomes enlightened. If anyone proclaims to be enlightened, simply nod your head and walk the other way.

~ David A. Bhodan

Enlightenment is total emptiness of mind. There is nothing you can do to get it. Any effort you make can only be an obstruction to it.

~ Ramesh Balsekar

I'm simply saying that there is a way to be sane. I'm saying that you can get rid of all this insanity created by the past in you. Just by being a simple witness of your thought processes.

It is simply sitting silently, witnessing the thoughts, passing before you. Just witnessing, not interfering not even judging, because the moment you judge you have lost the pure witness. The moment you say 'this is good, this is bad,' you have already jumped onto the thought process.

It takes a little time to create a gap between the witness and the mind. Once the gap is there, you are in for a great surprise, that you are not the mind, that you are the witness. A watcher.

And this process of watching is the very alchemy of real religion. Because as you become more and more deeply rooted in witnessing, thoughts start disappearing. You are, but the mind is utterly empty.

That's the moment of enlightenment. That is the moment that you become for the first time an unconditioned, sane, really free human being.

~ Osho

Enlightenment is a destructive process. It has nothing to do with becoming better or being happier. Enlightenment is the crumbling away of untruth. It's seeing through the facade of pretence. It's the complete eradication of everything we imagined to be true.

~ Adyashanti

The only time and place to find enlightenment is in this moment. No need to check your watch. The time is now.

~ Philip T. Sudo

Enlightenment Quotes & Passages

Strictly speaking, there are no enlightened people, there is only enlightened activity.

~ Shunryu Suzuki

chapter 9
Eternal Now

What actually happened was something absurdly simple and unspectacular: I stopped thinking. Reason and imagination and all mental chatter died down. For once, words really failed me.

Past and future dropped away. I forgot who and what I was, my name, manhood, animal-hood, all that could be called mine. It was as if I had been born that instant, brand new, mindless, innocent of all memories. There existed only the Now, that present moment and what was clearly given in it.

To look was enough. And what I found was khaki trouser legs terminating downwards in a pair of brown shoes, khaki sleeves terminating sideways in a pair of pink hands, and a khaki shirtfront terminating upwards in--absolutely nothing whatever! Certainly not in a head.

Enlightenment Quotes & Passages

It took me no time at all to notice that this nothing, this hole where a head should have been was no ordinary vacancy, no mere nothing. On the contrary, it was very much occupied. It was a vast emptiness vastly filled, a nothing that found room for everything - room for grass, trees, shadowy distant hills, and far above them snow peaks like a row of angular clouds riding the blue sky. I had lost a head and gained a world.

~ Douglas Harding

Most of us assume as a matter of common sense that space is nothing, that it's not important and has no energy. But as a matter of fact, space is the basis of existence. How could you have stars without space? Stars shine out of space and something comes out of nothing just in the same way as when you listen, in an unprejudiced way, you hear all sounds coming out of silence. It is amazing. Silence is the origin of sound just as space is the origin of stars, and woman is the origin of man. If you listen and pay close attention to what is, you will discover that there is no past, no future, and no one listening. You cannot hear yourself listening. You live in the eternal now and you are that. It is really extremely simple, and that is the way it is.

~ Alan Watts

To Awaken The Buddha Within

Why does the mind habitually deny or resist the Now? Because it cannot function and remain in control without time, which is past and future, so it perceives the timeless Now as threatening. Time and mind are in fact inseparable.

~ Eckhart Tolle

If you want to know what it means to be happy, look at a flower, a bird, a child; they are perfect images of the kingdom. For they live from moment to moment in the eternal now with no past and no future.

~ Anthony de Mello

Realization is uncovering that you are already Free. It is always Here and only relieves you of bondage. It is throwing the bucket of your individuality into the Well of Being, without the ropes of desire, intention, thought, or attachment.

Don't try to go anywhere, just simply Be. The only 'need' is to BE, not even seeing. It is so simple that it is difficult. It is Here and Now this very Instant.

There is no today, yesterday or tomorrow in Now. When nothing ever existed what is there to be free from? Emptiness has to be emptied of emptiness, Freedom must be free of freedom.

In Freedom there is nothing to do and nothing not to do. It cannot be imagined or touched. Human birth is for this Freedom, so smell freedom, inhale Freedom, Be Freedom. Every moment Freedom is Here to hug you.

Eternity is Now, living moment to moment.

~ Papaji

Time isn't precious at all, because it is an illusion. What you perceive as precious is not time, but the one point that is out of time: the Now. That is precious indeed.

The more you are focused on time-past and future-the more you miss the Now, the most precious thing there is.

~ Eckhart Tolle

Know that in this way there are myriads of forms and hundreds of grasses throughout the entire earth, and yet each grass and each form itself is the entire earth.

The study of this is the beginning of practice. When you are at this place, there is just one grass, there is just one form; there is understanding of form and no-understanding of form; there is understanding of grass and no-understanding of grass. Since there is nothing but just this moment, the time-being is all the time there is. Grass-being, form-being, are both time.

Each moment is all being, is the entire world. Reflect now whether any being or any world is left out of the present moment.

~ Dogen

Life can be found only in the present moment. The past is gone, the future is not yet here, and if we do not go back to ourselves in the present moment, we can't be in touch with life.

~ Thich Nhat Hanh

chapter 10
Non-duality

You are total unicity beyond duality. That you are. You are so one with yourself that you cannot perceive yourself. You can only imagine that you are other than that. It is like a knife that can cut so many vegetables but cannot cut itself because it is one with itself, or the scale which can weigh so many objects but cannot weigh itself.

It is the same with the one supreme Self, the sole Reality, being ever One with itself, it cannot perceive that which it Is; it can only perceive what it is not.

~ Mooji

Though others may talk of the Way of the Buddhas as something to be reached by various pious practices and by sutra-study, you must have nothing to do with such ideas. A perception, sudden as blinking, that subject and object are one, will lead to a deeply mysterious wordless understanding; and by this understanding will you awake to the truth of Zen.

~ Huang Po

When your mind doesn't stir inside, the world doesn't arise outside. When the world and the mind are both transparent, this is true vision. And such understanding is

~ Bodhidharma

The choice-less Truth of who you are is revealed to be permanently here permeating everything. Not a thing and not separate from anything.

~ Gangaji

For every individual is a unique manifestation of the Whole, as every branch is a particular outreaching of the tree. To manifest individuality, every branch must have a sensitive connection with the tree, just as our independently moving and differentiated fingers must have a sensitive connection with the whole body. The point, which can hardly be repeated too often, is that differentiation is not separation.

~ Alan Watts

I went looking for Him
And lost myself;
The drop merged with the Sea.
Who can find it now?

~Kabir

In the stillness of the night, the Goddess whispers. In the bright of the day, dear God roars. Life pulses, mind imagines, emotions wave, thoughts wander. What are these but the endless movements of One Taste, forever at play with its own gestures, whispering quietly to all who will listen: is this not yourself?

When the thunder roars, do you not hear your Self? When the lightening cracks, do you not see your Self? When the clouds float quietly across the sky, is this not your very own limitless Being, waving back at you?

~ Ken Wilber

Looking at a sunset, just for a second you forget your separateness: you are the sunset. That is the moment when you feel the beauty of it. But the moment you say that it is a beautiful sunset, you are no longer feeling it; you have come back to your separate, enclosed entity of the ego.

Now the mind is speaking. And this is one of the mysteries, that the mind can speak, and knows nothing; and the heart knows everything, and cannot speak. Perhaps to know too much makes it difficult to speak; the mind knows so little, it is possible for it to speak.

~ Osho

We live in succession, in division, in parts, in particles. Meantime within man is the soul of the whole; the wise silence; the universal beauty, to which every part and particle is equally related, the eternal ONE. And this deep power in which we exist and whose beatitude is all accessible to us, is not only self-sufficing and perfect in every hour, but the act of seeing and the thing seen, the seer and the spectacle, the subject and the object, are one. We see the world piece by piece, as the sun, the moon, the animal, the tree; but the whole, of which these are shining parts, is the soul.

~ Ralph Waldo Emerson

It can be made only when one recognizes the ground of being itself, when one recognizes directly that One is All.

~ Amit Goswami

All religions postulate the three fundamentals: the world, the soul and God; but it is the One Reality that manifests itself as these three. One can say: 'The three are really three' only so long as the ego lasts. Therefore to inhere in one's own Being, when the ego is dead is the perfect state.

The world is 'real', 'No, it is mere illusory appearance', 'The world is conscious,' 'No', 'The world is happiness', 'No,' -- What use is it to argue this? That state is agreeable to all wherein, having given up the objective outlook, one knows one's Self and loses all notions either of unity or duality, of oneself and the ego.

If one has form oneself, the world and God will also appear to have form; but if one is formless, who is to see these forms, and how? Without the eye can any object be seen?

The seeing Self is the Eye, and that Eye is the Eye of Infinity.

~ Ramana Maharshi

There is a Reality which is Indivisible, One, Alone, the Source and Being of all; not a thing, nor even a mind, but pure Spirit or clear Consciousness; and we are That and nothing but That, for That is our true Nature; and the only way to find It is to look steadily within, where are to be found utmost peace, unfading joy, and eternal life itself.

~ Douglas Harding

Just a look, just a touch and all worlds fall away.
Melting into one.
Falling into the other.
Never been separate.
Oneness beyond all appearances.

Enlightenment Quotes & Passages

All boundaries are meaningless.

All concepts, ridiculous.

No me, no you.

No inside, no outside.

~ Unmani

They said to Him: 'Shall we then, being children, enter the Kingdom?' Jesus said to them: 'When you make the two one, and when you make the inner as the outer and the outer as the inner and the above as the below, and when you make the male and the female into a single one, then you shall enter the kingdom.'

~ Jesus

The Ocean cannot stay alone and so the notion of wave is created. When waves rise Ocean loses nothing and when waves fall ocean gains nothing. Samsara, the illusion, Maya, the play, is the wave on the Ocean of Nirvana.

Waves are not separate from the Ocean, rays are not separate from the Sun, You are not separate from Existence-Consciousness-Bliss. This is a reflection on That.

~ Papaji

The same Consciousness prevails at rest as the Absolute and in motion as duality. When the sense of 'me' disappears completely, duality vanishes in ecstasy.

~ Ramesh Balsekar

chapter 11
Truth

Consider the possibility that Life is complete as it is, and that within each moment, Reality is infinitely manifesting. All the apparent parts are nothing other than an expression of one magnificent Whole--and You Are That

~ David A. Bhodan

WE ALREADY HAVE everything we need. There is no need for self-improvement. All these trips that we lay on ourselves--the heavy-duty fearing that we're bad and hoping that we're good, the identities that we so dearly cling to, the rage, the jealousy and the addictions of all kinds-- never touch our basic wealth. They are like clouds that temporarily block the sun. But all the time our warmth and brilliance are right here. This is who we really are. We are one blink of an eye away from being fully awake.

~ Pema Chodron

The only truth is I AM--I Exist. That is the only truth. Everything else is a concept. Rebirth is a concept. Your karma is a concept.

~ Ramesh Balsekar

If what you seek is Truth, there is one thing you must have above all else. 'I know. An overwhelming passion for it.' No. An unremitting readiness to admit you may be wrong.

~ Anthony de Mello

The Truth is inseparable from who you are. Yes, you are the Truth. If you look for it elsewhere, you will be deceived every time.

~ Eckhart Tolle

Enlightenment Quotes & Passages

Truth is by nature self-evident. As soon as you remove the cobwebs of ignorance that surround it, it shines clear.

~ Mahatma Gandi

You can stop telling your story in less than an instant. Even if it is a good story, stop indulging the telling of it and immediately the truth can be experienced. The possibility is to recognize that all our stories, however complex and multi-layered, however deeply implanted in our genetic structure, are only stories. The truth of who you are is not a story. The vastness and the closeness of that truth precedes all stories. When you overlook the Truth of who you are in allegiance to some story, you miss a precious opportunity for self-recognition.

~ Gangaji

Truth is not something outside to be discovered, it is something inside to be realized.

~ Osho

The timeless non-state cannot be achieved because the mind cannot evolve towards it. The mind can only bring you to the threshold. Awakening comes unexpectedly when you do not wait for it, when you live in not-knowing. Only then are you available.

~ Jean Klein

Truth is not a reward for good behavior, nor a prize for passing some tests. It cannot be brought about. It is the primary, the unborn, the ancient source of all that is. You are eligible because you are. You need not merit truth. It is your own. Stand still, be quiet.

~ Nisargadatta Maharaj

When you realize that nothing, no 'thing', ever has the power to make you permanently happy, you receive a deeper invitation: to realize that nothing, the no-thing that you are, IS the source of true happiness.

~ Jeff Foster

Enlightenment Quotes & Passages

A man may be born, but in order to be born he must first die, and in order to die he must first awake.

~ Gurdjieff

Brahman or the Self is like a cinema screen and the world like the pictures on it. You can see the picture only so long as there is a screen.

But when the observer himself becomes the screen only the Self remains.

~ Ramana Maharshi

All the religions of the world, while they may differ in other respects, unitedly proclaim that nothing lives in this world but Truth.

~ Mahatma Gandi

chapter 12
Illusion

It's an illusion that 'you' exist--the entity 'you' is imagined. The imagination that 'you' exist as something or someone separate is the cause of acceptance or rejection of something known. It is illusion telling the story of its own deception. The knower and the known are just concepts seemingly dividing natural, non-conceptual knowing. Believing in the thought 'I am' gives seeming reality to the objective world which is constantly changing, yet everything in essence is that changeless natural knowing--nothing else.

~ Sailor Bob Adamson

Do not repeat after me words that you do not understand. Do not merely put on a mask of my ideas, for it will be an illusion and you will thereby deceive yourself.

~ Jiddu Krishnamurti

Enlightenment Quotes & Passages

We loosely talk of Self-realization, for lack of a better term. But how can one realize or make real that which alone is real? All we need to do is to give up our habit of regarding as real that which is unreal. All religious practices are meant solely to help us do this. When we stop regarding the unreal as real, then reality alone will remain, and we will be that.

~ Ramana Maharshi

Oneness plays the game of being two, asleep, looking for oneness. When awakening happens, it is only the dropping away of taking two-ness seriously; that's all we're talking about here. This whole thing is as simple as this--all that's in the way of awakening is a false idea. It really is. It's a pretence which you've been conditioned to believe. And when the idea that you are two drops away, there is Oneness.

~ Tony Parsons

The thinking mind, the ego and the me are all the same. They are different names for the same thing, which is an illusion.

~ Ramesh Balsekar

Just as it is known, that an image of one's face is seen, depending on a mirror, but does not really exist as a face, so the conception of 'I' exists, dependent on mind and body, but like the image of a face, the 'I' does not at all exist as its own reality.

~ Nagarjuna

We live in illusion and the appearance of things. There is a reality. We are that reality. When you understand this, you see that you are nothing, and being nothing, you are everything. That is all.

~ Kalu Rinpoche

Happiness is our natural state. Happiness is the natural state of little children, to whom the kingdom belongs until they have been polluted and contaminated by the stupidity of society and culture. To acquire happiness you don't have to do anything, because happiness cannot be acquired.

Does anybody know why? Because we have it already. How can you acquire what you already have? Then why don't you experience it? Because you've got to drop something. You've got to drop illusions. You don't have to add anything in order to be happy; you've got to drop something.

Life is easy, life is delightful. It's only hard on your illusions, your ambitions, your greed, your cravings. Do you know where these things come from? From having identified with all kinds of labels!

~ Anthony de Mello

Whoever realizes that the six senses aren't real, that the five aggregates are fictions,

that no such things can be located anywhere in the body, understands the language of Buddha's.

~ Bodhidharma

To Awaken The Buddha Within

Like a magician's illusions, dreams and a moon reflected in water, all beings and their environments are empty of inherent existence. Though not solidly existent, all these appear, like water bubbles coming forth in water.

~ Gung Tang

Presently you think you are mixed up with the mind and are trying to disentangle yourself from the turmoil of thoughts.

But both the mind and the one trying to disentangle itself share the same unreality. Both are imagined inside the Unchanging. What perceives this is the Real.

~ Mooji

The description is not the described; I can describe the mountain, but the description is not the mountain, and if you are caught up in the description, as most people are, then you will never see the mountain.

~ Jiddu Krishnamurti

Enlightenment Quotes & Passages

Do you know that even when you look at a tree and say, `That is an oak tree', or `that is a banyan tree', the naming of the tree, which is botanical knowledge, has so conditioned your mind that the word comes between you and actually seeing the tree? To come in contact with the tree you have to put your hand on it and the word will not help you to touch it.

~ Jiddu Krishnamurti

All philosophies are mental fabrications. There has never been a single doctrine by which one could enter the true essence of things.

~ Nagarjuna

chapter 13
Fear

To remain stable is to refrain from trying to separate yourself from a pain because you know that you cannot. Running away from fear is fear, fighting pain is pain, trying to be brave is being scared. If the mind is in pain, the mind is pain. The thinker has no other form than his thought. There is no escape.

~ Alan Watts

If a man considers that he is born, he cannot avoid the fear of death. Let him find out if he has been born or if the Self has any birth. He will discover that the Self always exists, that the body that is born resolves itself into thought and that the emergence of thought is the root of all mischief. Find from where thoughts emerge.

Enlightenment Quotes & Passages

Then you will be able to abide in the ever-present inmost Self and be free from the idea of birth or the fear of death.

~ Ramana Maharshi

Fear is a natural reaction to moving closer to the Truth.

~ Pema Chodron

To be fully alive, fully human, and completely awake is to be continually thrown out of the nest. To live fully is to be always in no-man's-land, to experience each moment as completely new and fresh.

The fear of anything is the fear of death, and thefear of death is the same as the fear of life. You cannot live fully until you are willing to die fully and you cannot die fully until you are willing to meet the fear of death fully. If you really meet the fear of death, you are at peace. You recognize what cannot die. To meet death is not suicide, nor is it the least bit dangerous. It only seems dangerous. What is dangerous, what is a living suicide, is to live your life in bondage to the belief that you are limited to a body (or a mind, or anything). As long as you resist the fact of death and hide from death through the tricks of the mind, you will suffer.

~ Gangaji

chapter 14
Love

There is one thing I can tell you for sure. All is well. Everything is unfolding as it should. I can tell you that truly nothing is wrong anywhere. If you think you have a problem, that's the mistake--thinking you have a problem. As soon as you stop thinking, everything will go right.

~ Robert Adams

Always say 'Yes' to the present moment. What could be more futile, more insane, than to create inner resistance to what already is?

Truly it is one of the unforeseen pleasures of the 1st-Person life to gaze unabashed into the faces of one's friends, without feeling or thinking anything in particular, and just see them for what they always were--things for looking at and never for looking out of.

This isn't an unloving state, reducing you to a cardboard cut-out. Quite the reverse; it is a most loving refusal to separate my Consciousness from yours, and it removes the last barrier between us. Liberated from the superstition of plural spirits, we are at last really one. This is the perfect love which casts out fear--the fear inseparable from living in a haunted world.

~ Douglas Harding

Love is the recognition of oneness in a world of duality. This is the birth of God into the world of form. Love makes the world less worldly, less dense, more transparent to the divine dimension, the light of consciousness itself.

~ Eckhart Tolle

Aloneness simply means completeness. You are whole; there is no need of anybody else to complete you. So try to find out your innermost center where you are always alone, have always been alone. In life, in death--wherever you are--you will be alone.

But it is so full! It is not empty; it is so full and so complete and so overflowing with all the juices of life, with all the beauties and benedictions of existence, that once you have tasted your aloneness, the pain in the heart will disappear. Instead, a new rhythm of tremendous sweetness, peace, joy, bliss, will be there.

~ Osho

The consciousness in you and the consciousness in me, apparently two, really one, seek unity and that is love.

~ Nisargadatta Maharaj

The only thing that is Eternal is Love. This Love *is* the Beloved *and* the Lover. You are not to make any efforts in this relationship. When you are in front of your Beloved, this Beloved will not ask you to make any effort. This Beloved will take care of you and whatever she does you will accept it. At that time you will not think what is going on because in Love, there is no dialogue.

In Love there is no dialogue, no question, no answer. Simply both are quiet. You are quiet and your Beloved is quiet and something great is about to happen Now. You have to wait.

When you don't make any separation between the Beloved and the Lover you have found the secret: That you have never been separated from anything. This is all you have to do. Did you get this secret?

~ Papaji

Honor everything, let everything be exactly the way it is.. Honor all, and leave all alone. Let pain persist. Allow rage to roar, tension to taunt, and anxiety to annihilate. If you can do this, all the illusory guards blocking God will die. What will be left, my friend, is the fearless state. The end of the fear of love.

~ Stuart Schwartz

This absolute intimacy of pure experiencing is what we call love. It is the absence of distance, separation or otherness. There is no room for two there. Love is the experience of pure non-duality.

~ Rupert Spira

Wisdom tells me I am nothing. Love tells me I am everything. And between the two my life flows.

~ Nisargadatta Maharaj

No matter what happens in a movie, the movie screen is not affected. When the main character ages, the screen doesn't age. When time passes on the screen, time never passes for the screen. When the main character dies, the screen remains, and is not diminished. Even when the movie ends, the screen does not end, it just remains open for the next movie--a comedy, a horror, a romance, a silent movie from 1912, a 3D blockbuster from 2012--whatever it will be.

The screen accepts it all Movie or no movie at all. The screen never fights the movie, nor does it cling to it. It has no name, no age, no identity of its own, but allows all those wonderful identities to parade themselves about, asking nothing in return. It is rarely appreciated, often ignored, but absolutely essential for the relative dance of life.

The screen is pure love. It is what you are. Now, who wants to see a movie?

~ Jeff Foster

Those who see worldly life as an obstacle to Dharma see no Dharma in everyday actions; they have not yet discovered that there are no everyday actions outside of Dharma.

~ Dogen

chapter 15
Suffering

Suffering is a sign that you're out of touch with the truth. Suffering is given to you that you might open your eyes to the truth, that you might understand that there's falsehood somewhere, just as physical pain is given to you so you will understand that there is disease or illness somewhere.

Suffering points out that there is falsehood somewhere. Suffering occurs when you clash with reality. When your illusions clash with reality when your falsehoods clash with the truth, then you have suffering. Otherwise, there is no suffering.

~ Anthony de Mello

To Awaken The Buddha Within

If the doors of perception were cleansed, everything would appear to man as it is, infinite. For man has closed himself up, till he sees all things through narrow chinks of his cavern.

~ William Blake

Why are you unhappy? Because 99.9% of everything you think, and of everything you do is for yourself. And there isn't one.

~ Wei Wu Wei

If peace comes from seeing the whole, then misery stems from a loss of perspective.

We begin so aware and grateful. The sun somehow hangs there in the sky. The little bird sings. The miracle of life just happens. Then we stub our toe, and in that moment of pain, the whole world is reduced to our poor little toe. Now, for a day or two, it is difficult to walk. With every step, we are reminded of our poor little toe.

Our vigilance becomes: Which defines our day-- the pinch we feel in walking on a bruised toe, or the miracle still happening?

Enlightenment Quotes & Passages

It is the giving over to smallness that opens us to misery. In truth, we begin taking nothing for granted, grateful that we have enough to eat, that we are well enough to eat. But somehow, through the living of our days, our focus narrows like a camera that shutters down, cropping out the horizon, and one day we're miffed at a diner because the eggs are runny or the hash isn't seasoned just the way we like.

When we narrow our focus, the problem seems everything. We forget when we were lonely, dreaming of a partner. We forget first beholding the beauty of another. We forget the comfort of first being seen and held and heard. When our view shuts down, we're up in the night annoyed by the way our lover pulls the covers or leaves the dishes in the sink without soaking them first.

In actuality, misery is a moment of suffering allowed to become everything. So, when feeling miserable, we must look wider than what hurts. When feeling a splinter, we must, while trying to remove it, remember there is a body that is not splinter, and a spirit that is not splinter, and a world that is not splinter.

~ Mark Nepo

Not to be able to stop thinking is a dreadful affliction, but we don't realize this because almost everybody is suffering from it, so it is considered normal. This incessant mental noise prevents you from finding that realm of inner stillness that is inseparable from Being.

~ Eckhart Tolle

The tragedy of an attachment is that if its object is not attained it causes unhappiness. But if it is attained, it does not cause happiness--it merely causes a flash of pleasure followed by weariness, and it is always accompanied, of course, by the anxiety that you may lose the object of your attachment.

~ Anthony de Mello

Before you embark on a journey of revenge, dig two graves.

~ Confucius

chapter 16
Death

The death of the body/mind is only the ending of the illusion of a journey in time.

The awakening to unconditional love is immediate. We are enveloped in our original nature regardless of anything that apparently happened.

When the body/mind is dropped, there is no intermediary process of preparation or purification. How can there be? Who was there? All ideas of a personal 'afterlife' or reincarnation are merely the mind wishing to preserve the illusion of it's continuity.

The story is over. The divine novel has been written, and regardless of how the mind might judge, not one iota could have been different. The scenery evaporates and the characters have left the stage--their apparent existence begins and ends with the dream that has been played out.

For we are the ocean and the waves, the darkness and the light.

~ Tony Parsons

Many have died; you also will die. The drum of death is being beaten. The world has fallen in love with a dream. Only sayings of the wise will remain.

~ Kabir

The reason why everyone wants to avoid death is because Eternity is our real nature.

Death is not to be feared because it is an enjoyable and happy occasion and it only hurts one who has anger, greed, attraction and aversion. Death only comes to an active mind. Even the gods must face death.

All die but there is no grief because the Indweller lives. Death is only the five elements returning to themselves.

Enlightenment Quotes & Passages

The essence of wave, ocean and raindrop is still water: Nothing can be lost. When a raindrop touches the ocean it becomes ocean. So do not fear death for nothing can ever be lost and nothing can ever be gained.

Death only takes those who have become something, death only takes the body, the dress.

Death is a foolish notion.

~ Papaji

Look deeply into the idea that you are a separate entity navigating as best as 'you' can, treading safely (or adventurously) to 'your' eventual demise. Consider the possibility who you really are has never been a limited, finite being with a certain life span, here to live for a while only to die.

~ David A. Bhodan

Death is a stripping away of all that is not you. The secret of life is to 'die before you die'-- and find that there is no death.

~ Eckhart Tolle

For certain is death for the born, and certain is birth for the dead; Therefore over the inevitable, Thou shouldst not grieve.

~ Bhagavad Gita

When this life force leaves the body, it will not seek permission from anything. It came spontaneously and will leave spontaneously. That is all that happens in what is called death. Death is the culmination of the experience 'I am'. After the termination of the 'I amness' there is no experience of knowingness or not knowingness. What did you know prior to your birth? Similarly, after death this instrument is missing; without the body there is no experience. Eternity has no birth and no death, but a temporary state has a beginning and an end.

Even when the consciousness goes, you prevail--you always are--as the Absolute. As the consciousness you are everything that comes into manifestation. Whatever is, is you. But, when you fully understand the knowledge 'I am' and all its manifestations, then you will understand that, in truth, you are not that. You are the unlimited, which is not susceptible to the senses.

Enlightenment Quotes & Passages

By limiting yourself to the body you have closed yourself to the unlimited potential which you really are. Treat the body like a visitor or a guest, which has come and which will go. You must know your position as a host very clearly while it is still here, and while it is here you must also know what your position will be after it leaves.

In spirituality there is no question of doing... only observing and understanding. But, if you try to understand spirituality through various concepts, like birth and rebirth, you will get caught up in them in a vicious cycle. And once you are caught up in them you are bound to have them.

Out of concepts the forms are created. Right now, think of that last moment when the body will go-- at that time with what identity are you going to quit? When you become aware of your true nature, then at the end of your life you will not be prepared to give even one paisa to extend your life. You will have lost all love for this manifested world and you will not want even this consciousness for five minutes more.

The vital breath leaves the body, the 'I amness' recedes and goes to the Absolute. That is the greatest moment, the moment of immortality. The 'I amness' was there, the movement was there, and now it is extinguished. Being alive is never as an individual, but simply being part of the spontaneous manifestation. Now that has subsided in death.

The ignorant one will struggle and get frightened at the moment of death; most reluctantly he will give up the consciousness to a concept he has come to call time. But the Jnani gives up the beingness to his own true nature; for him it is the happiest of moments.

~ Nisargadatta Maharaj

Whatever you want your death to be, let first your life be exactly the same--because death is not separate from life. Death is not an end to life, but only a change. Life continues, has continued, will always continue. But forms become useless, old, more a burden than a joy; then it is better to give life a new, fresh form.

Death is a blessing, it is not a curse.

~ Osho

Suppressing the fear of death makes it all the stronger. The point is only to know, beyond any shadow of doubt, that 'I' and all other 'things' now present will vanish, until this knowledge compels you to release them--to know it now as surely as if you had just fallen off the rim of the Grand Canyon.

Enlightenment Quotes & Passages

Indeed you were kicked off the edge of a precipice when you were born, and it's no help to cling to the rocks falling with you. If you are afraid of death, be afraid. The point is to get with it, to let it take over--fear, ghosts, pains, transience, dissolution, and all. And then comes the hitherto unbelievable surprise; you don't die because you were never born. You had just forgotten who you are.

~ Alan Watts

Death--the last sleep? No, it is the final awakening.

~ Walter Scott

We rather cling to the known than face the unknown, the known being our loneliness, our sorrow, our embittered existence. And as we cannot face that thing called death, we invent all kinds of theories; in the East reincarnation, here resurrection, or whatever it is.

~ Krishnamurti

It was not born; It will never die: nor once having been, can it ever cease to be: Unborn, Eternal, Ever-enduring, yet Most Ancient, the Spirit dies not when the body is dead.

~ Lord Krishna

Life and death are two sides of the same coin. Without death, there is no life. What could be more natural than the physical death of something that is born to die? What could be more natural than the death of that which was never meant for eternal life?

~ David A. Bhodan

Whoever finds the interpretation of these sayings will not experience death.

~ Jesus

The body dies. This means what? It means only the thought 'I am', that concept, has disappeared. Nothing has happened to the knower of the whole happening. So long as the basic concept 'I am' is there, the conceptual element cannot disappear.

It is the concept itself that has given various names to itself, but it is still the same concept. Before this concept of 'I am' came on you, were you happy or unhappy? Was there even any feeling of happiness or unhappiness or any of the dualities? In the absence of the basic concept 'I am', there is no thought, no awareness, and no consciousness of one's existence.

~ Nisargadatta Maharaj

It sometimes happens that one who is on a spiritual path, or even who has not yet begun consciously seeking, has a glimpse of Realization during which, for a brief eternity, he experiences absolute certainty of his divine, immutable, universal Self. Such an experience came to the Maharshi when he was a lad of sixteen. He himself has described it:

It was about six weeks before I left Madurai for good that the great change in my life took place. It was quite sudden. I was sitting alone in a room on the first floor of my uncle's house. I seldom had any sickness, and on that day there was nothing wrong with my health, but a sudden violent fear of death overtook me.

There was nothing in my state of health to account for it, and I did not try to account for it or to find out whether there was any reason for the fear. I just felt 'I am going to die' and began thinking what to do about it. It did not occur to me to consult a doctor, or my elders or friends; I felt that I had to solve the problem myself, there and then.

The shock of the fear of death drove my mind inwards and I said to myself mentally, without actually framing the words: Now death has come; what does it mean?

What is it that is dying?

The body dies. And I at once dramatized the occurrence of death. I lay with my limbs stretched out stiff as though rigor mortis had set in, and imitated a corpse so as to give greater reality to the enquiry. I held my breath and kept my lips tightly closed so that no sound could escape, so that neither the word 'I' nor any other word could be uttered.

Well then, I said to myself, this body is dead. It will be carried stiff to the burning ground and there burnt and reduced to ashes. But with the death of this body am I dead? Is the body I? It is silent and inert but I feel the full force of my personality and even the voice of the 'I' within me, apart from it. So I am Spirit transcending the body. The body dies but the Spirit that transcends it cannot be touched by death. That means I am the deathless Spirit.

Enlightenment Quotes & Passages

All this was not dull thought; it flashed through me vividly as living Truth which I perceived directly, almost without thought-process. 'I' was something very real, the only real thing about my present state, and all the conscious activity connected with my body was centered on that 'I'.

From that moment onwards the 'I' or Self, focused attention on Itself by a powerful fascination. Fear of death had vanished once and for all. Absorption in the Self continued unbroken from that time on.

~ Ramana Maharshi

chapter 17
Just This

All there is, is this perception. Perception is not owned by a someone or by a body/mind. Perception just is. All that is perceived, is just appearing in perception. All appearances are simply perception, including the appearance of this body/mind or that chair. There is no separation.

I am absolutely alone. There are no others. There is not even a character 'me'. The character 'me' is also a perception. Thoughts are perceived. Emotions are perceived. It is all perceived. What perceives is Life itself. Life perceives the whole play. I am life and as this, I am the play of whatever happens.

Closed eyes and there is only nothing. There is only sensation felt in nothing. This nothing is the emptiness in which everything happens. This nothing is alive. Open eyes and there is a rush of perception. Nothing overflows as everything. Eyes closed or open, the fabric of life is alive nothingness.

~ Unmani

So close you can't see it. So deep you can't fathom it. So simple you can't believe it. So good you can't accept it.

~ Kalu Rinpoche

Since every wave in the ocean is 'made of' the ocean itself, since it has the same 'substance' as the ocean, pushing away a wave of yourself--a thought, a sensation, a feeling, a sound--numbing yourself to it, rejecting it, denying it, trying to escape it--is equivalent to pushing away the entire essence of the ocean. Pushing away a moment of sadness, or pain, or doubt, or fear, or joy, or delight, is the same as pushing away all of life.

Even the smallest wave, in essence, is as vast as the ocean--there are no insignificant thoughts or feelings, no 'ordinary' experiences, no moments unworthy of kind attention. All is consciousness-- or if you prefer, all is God--beyond all our limited and outdated ideas of what those words mean. Even the smallest wave is sacred, here in the vast open space that you are. As Jesus said, 'Whatever you do unto the least of these, you do unto Me', and perhaps he was talking about You.

~ Jeff Foster

Earth and sky, woods and fields, lakes and rivers, the mountain and the sea, are excellent schoolmasters, and teach some of us more than we can ever learn from books.

~ John Lubbock

Self shining presence-awareness is not the result of effort. There is no need to try to do something with the expectation that suddenly awareness will be there.

Presence-awareness is always here and now whether it is recognized or seemingly lost. It is not something that can be created or destroyed.

Conceptual thinking is like the cloud that seemingly blocks the sun. Being at ease in non-conceptual naturalness is presence awareness already here and now.

Recognize again, and again, and again, and the knowing it is always so is constant in spite of what appears and disappears. Self-knowing, self-shining--just this, nothing else.

~ Sailor Bob Adamson

You do not have to wait for grace to take place--it has already taken place and is taking place in you. You have been given an interest in your true nature--that is the most valuable thing you could have been given. That is grace. Say 'Yes' to the gift you've been given and follow it.

~ Rupert Spira

I exist as I am, that is enough. If no other in the world be aware I sit content, and if each and all be aware I sit content. One world is aware, and by the far the largest to me, and that is myself.

~ Walt Whitman

There is no one that can do anything and there is nothing that needs to be done or known! There never has been anyone to do anything. The whole misconception that keeps us firmly in the sense of being separate is the idea that we can do anything or the idea that we need to do anything. Why do we need to do anything? There is just what's happening. It is all immaculately complete and without need.

~ Tony Parsons

I AM not speaking to any 'body'.

I AM not speaking to any 'mind'.

I AM speaking to THAT I AM that I AM.

That PRESENCE AWARENESS, that expresses through the mind as the thought I AM.

Just THIS, NOTHING else.

~ Sailor Bob Adamson

The Deathless, Eternal Presence or Awareness that is already Buddha or Pure Mind is fully available in any state or stage of consciousness, including your own present state of awareness right now.

So I'm going to talk you into this state, or try to, using what are known as 'pointing out instructions.' I am not going to try to get you into a different state of consciousness, or an altered state of consciousness, or a non-ordinary state. I am going to simply point out something that is already occurring in you own, present, ordinary, natural state.

So let's start by just being aware of the world around us. Look out there at the sky, and just relax your mind; let your mind and the sky mingle. Notice the clouds floating by in the sky. Notice that this takes no effort on your part. Your present awareness, in which all these clouds are floating, is very simple, very easy, effortless, spontaneously. You simply notice that there is an effortless awareness of the clouds. The same is true of those trees, and those birds, and those rocks. You simply and effortlessly witness them.

Look now at the sensations in your own body. You can be aware of whatever bodily feelings are present; perhaps pressure where you are sitting, perhaps warmth in your tummy, maybe tightness in you neck. But even if these feeling are tight and tense, you can easily be aware of them. These feelings arise in you present awareness, and that awareness is very simple, easy, effortless, spontaneous. You simply and effortlessly witness them.

Look at the thoughts arising in your mind. You might notice various images, symbols, concepts, desires, hopes and fears, all spontaneously arising in your awareness. They arise, stay a bit, and pass. These thoughts and feelings arise in your present awareness, and that awareness is very simple, effortless, spontaneous. You simply and effortlessly witness them.

So notice:

You can see the clouds float by because you are not those clouds--YOU are the witness of those clouds.

You can feel bodily feelings because you are not those feelings--YOU are the witness of those feelings.

You can see thoughts float by because you are not those thoughts--YOU are the witness of those thoughts.

Spontaneously and naturally, these things all arise, on their own, in your present, effortless awareness.

So who are you?

You are not objects out there, you are not feelings, you are not thoughts--you are effortlessly aware of those, so you are no those.

Who are what are you?

Say it this way to yourself: I have feelings, but I am not those feelings.

Who am I?

Enlightenment Quotes & Passages

I have thoughts, but I am not those thought.

Who am I?

I have desires, but I am not those desires.

Who am I?

So push back into the source of your own awareness. You push back into the Witness, and you rest in the Witness. I am not objects, not feelings, not desires, not thoughts. But then people usually make a big mistake. They think that if they rest in the Witness, they are going to see something or feel something neat and special. But you are won't see anything. If you see something, that is just another object, another feeling, another thought, another sensation, another image. But those are all objects; those are what you are not.

Now, as you rest in the Witness--realizing, I am not objects, I am not feelings, I am not thoughts--all you will notice is a sense of freedom, a sense of liberation, a sense of release--release from the terrible constriction of identifying with these puny little finite objects, your little body and little mind and little ego, all of which are objects that can be seen, and thus are not the true Seer, the real Self, the pure Witness, which is what you really are.

So you won't see anything in particular. Whatever is arising is fine. Clouds float by in the sky, feelings float by in the body, thoughts float by in the mind--and you can effortlessly witness all of them. The all spontaneously arise in your own present, easy, effortless awareness. And this witnessing awareness is not itself anything specific you can see. It is just a vast, background sense of freedom--or pure emptiness--and in that pure emptiness, which you are, the entire manifest world arises.

You are that freedom, openness, emptiness--and not any itty bitty thing that arises in it. Resting in that empty, free, easy, effortless witnessing, notice that the clouds are arising in the vast space of your awareness. The clouds are arising within you so much so, you can taste the clouds, you are one with the clouds. It is as if they are on this side of your skin, they are so close. The sky and your awareness have become one, and all things in the sky are floating effortlessly through your own awareness. You can kiss the sun, swallow the mountain, they are that close.

Zen says 'Swallow the Pacific Ocean in a single gulp', and that's the easiest thing in the world, when inside and outside are no longer two. When subject and object are non-dual, when the looker and looked at are One Taste.

You see?

~ Ken Wilber (Pointing Out Instructions)

Enlightenment Quotes & Passages

Author Index

Adyashanti: 4, 5, 22, 30, 32, 53, 57,

Alan Watts: 39, 42, 43, 60, 66, 83, 102

Amit Goswami: 68

Anthony de Mello: 30, 37, 61, 73, 80, 92, 95

Bhagavad Gita : 99

Bodhidharma: 31. 65, 81

Buddha: 17, 21, 39, 43

Charlotte J. Beck: 55

Chogyam Trungpa: 15, 54

Confucius: 95

David A. Bhodan: 10, 27, 51, 56, 72, 98, 103

Deepak Chopra: 46

Dogen: 2, 27, 52, 63, 91

Douglas Harding: 40, 60, 69, 87

Eckhart Tolle: 20, 22, 41, 47, 61, 73, 87, 95, 98

Gangaji: 4, 21, 25, 52, 65, 74, 85

Gung Tang: 81

Gurdjieff: 76

Enlightenment Quotes & Passages

Huang Po: 65
Jean Klein: 5, 25, 75

Jeff Foster: 75, 90, 109

Jiddu Krishnamurti: 3, 7, 38, 78, 81, 82

Jesus: 70, 103

John Lubbock: 109

John Wheeler: 10, 12, 14, 18, 46

Kabir: 66, 97

Kalu Rinpoche: 16, 79, 108

Ken Wilber: 9, 31, 67, 115

Krishnamurti: 102

Lao Tzu : 25, 41

Lord Krishna: 103

Mahatma Gandi: 74, 76

Mark Nepo: 94

Mooji: 12, 16, 23, 26, 28, 38, 44, 49, 64, 81

Muso Kokushi: 19

Nagarjuna: 79, 82

Nisargadatta Maharaj: 1, 3, 20, 28, 42, 45, 75, 88, 90, 101, 104

Osho: 21, 53, 54, 57, 67, 74, 88, 101

Papaji: 6, 11, 47, 62, 71, 89, 97

Pema Chodron: 15, 41, 73, 84

Philip T. Sudo: 57

Ralph Waldo Emerson: 20, 68

Ramana Maharshi:
3, 5, 7, 33, 69, 76, 78, 84, 106

Ramesh Balsekar:
31, 56, 71, 73, 79

Robert Adams: 14, 50, 55, 86

Rumi: 33, 34, 41, 45, 48

Rupert Spira: 36, 89, 1110

Sailor Bob Adamson: 2, 23, 50, 77, 110, 111

Shakesphere: 18

Shunryu Suzuki: 23, 58,

Stuart Schwartz: 89

Sogyal Rinpoche: 13

Thich Nhat Hanh: 63

Tony Parsons: 19, 34, 48, 78, 97, 111

Walter Scott: 102

Unmani: 33, 70, 108

Walt Whitman: 26, 40, 110

Wei Wu Wei: 29, 43, 93

William Blake: 93

Enlightenment Quotes & Passages

Made in the USA
Middletown, DE
15 April 2017